T H E
TREE·STUMP

Written by Chris Forbes ❧ Illustrated by Don Sullivan

📖 ScottForesman
A Division of HarperCollinsPublishers

4a

In went the mouse.

In went the squirrel.

3

In went the rabbit.

In went the raccoon.

In went the owl.

In went the porcupine.
Ouch!

Out came the animals.

Ow, Ow, Ow!